The
Christian
Spirit

The Christian Spirit

A Poetic Reflection on Philippians

H. C. Kim

The Hermit Kingdom Press

Cheltenham   Seoul   Bangalore   Cebu City

The Christian Spirit

A Poetic Reflection on Philippians

The Hermit Kingdom Press
7817 Gayl Road
Cheltenham, PA 19012

also,
Seoul, Korea
Bangalore, India
Cebu City, Philippines

ISBN: 0972386424

http://www.HCKim.org

I would like to dedicate these poems to Christians in India
- past, present, and future

Preface

I have often wondered what made St. Paul so dedicated to his Christian work. I marveled at the richness of his theology. I knew from the beginning the secret formula was for his love of Christ and His body, the Christian Church. But the more I read St. Paul's Epistles, the more I realize what that really means. Reading Philippines carefully and reflecting on the wonderful contents provided such an experience. I hope I have captured in my poetry at least a little bit of my spiritual experience. I wish that you can share in my poetic reflection and benefit spiritually by it.

H. C. Kim
Jesus College
Cambridge
United Kingdom

Acknowledgements

The poems contained in this volume were written primarily in Heidelberg, Germany, and Bangalore, India.

I would first like to thank the University of Cambridge for granting me leave to research at the Ruprecht-Karls-Universität Heidelberg during the Easter Term, 2002. I am also grateful for the support that the University of Cambridge provided for my teaching at the Asia Evangelical College and Seminary in Bangalore. I would particularly like to thank my college at the institution, Jesus College, for awarding me a grant from its Research Fund. The Faculty of Divinity also generously awarded me a grant from the McPherson Fund, for which I am thankful.

Secondly, I would like to thank Wissenschaftlich-Theologisches Seminar of the Ruprecht-Karls- Universität Heidelberg and one of its faculty members, Professor Gerd Theissen, for hosting me during my research stay in Germany. Professor Theissen was particularly kind and took me into his home for first two weeks of my stay in Heidelberg and that made the transition to a new place that much smoother. The library of the theology department and the central university library in the Old City provided important materials that added to my reflection. I would also like to thank the speakers and participants of the New Testament lecture series, many of them academics in their own right who will do fruitful research in Germany for years to come.

Thirdly, I would like to thank Asia Evangelical College and Seminary and its president, the Rev. Dr. Y. John Chung for inviting me as a visiting professor. I have benefited from their kind hospitality, and I hope that my teaching at the institution benefited its members at least in some small way. I would also like to thank the master's degree students of my intensive summer course, "Theology according to Jesus of Nazareth," for their diligence and inquisitive questions. These students from all over India and from neighboring countries, like Nepal, made my teaching experience enjoyable. Asia Evangelical College and Seminary is certainly a benefit to India and the religion.

Table of Contents

"Servants Of Christ Jesus"   17

"The Source Of Peace"   20

"To Be Remembered With Thanksgiving"   22

"Partnership In The Gospel"   23

"Completion"   24

"Defending And Confirming The Gospel"   26

"Love Abounding Knowledge"   28

"To Advance The Gospel"   30

"I Am In Chains For Christ"   31

"Because Of My Chains"   34

"Motives Do Not Matter"   36

"Those Who Preach Out Of Good Will"   39

"Hostile Motives"   41

"I Rejoice"   44

"My Deliverance"   46

"Whether By Life Or By Death"   48

"For To Me"   51

"Fruitful Labor"   53

"To Be With Christ"   55

"For You, I remain"   56

"The Conviction"   58

"Joy To Go Around"   61

"Contending As One Man"   62

"Like A Good Coach"   64

"Embrace Pain"   66

"One In Spirit And Purpose"   68

"Christian Humility"   71

"The Interests Of Others"   73

"The Attitude Of Christ"   75

"In Very Nature God"   77

"Being Made In Human Likeness"   80

"Obedient To Death"   82

"God Exalted Himself"   84

"Every Knee Should Bow"   86

"Every Tongue Confess"   88

"Work Out Your Salvation"   90

"Hold Out The Word Of Life"   93

"A Drink Offering"   94

"Hope In The Lord Jesus"   96

"Genuine Interest"   97

"Looking Out For Self-Interest"   99

"The Apple Does Not Fall Far From The Tree"   100

"First Timothy, Then Me"   101

"Fellow Soldier"   103

"Anxiety"   105

"Honor Men Like Him" 107

"Value In Repetition" 108

"Watch Out For Those Dogs!" 110

"Legalistic Righteousness" 112

"Past Profit Is Current Loss" 113

"Righteousness By Faith" 114

"I Want To Know Christ" 115

"Looking Forward To Glorification" 117

"To Win The Prize" 118

"Mature Christians Should Think Like Me" 120

"Enemies Of The Cross" 122

"The Destiny Of The Enemies Of The Cross" 124

"Our Citizenship Is In Heaven" 126

"My Joy And Crown" 128

"Agree With Each Other In The Lord" 129

"The Transcendent Peace Of God" 131

"God Of Spiritual Peace Be With You" 132

"Expression" 134

"Contentment In Need" 136

"Through Him Who Gives Me Strength" 138

"Financial Support" 139

"Fragrant Offering" 140

"Glorious Riches In Christ" 141

"Glory Forever And Ever" 142

"Caesar's Household" 143

"Servants Of Christ Jesus"
Philippians 1:1

Identity markers are important
Who are you?
How do you perceive yourself?
What do others think about you?
These questions are pictures of one's *Weltanshauung*

Paul and Timothy
Inspired authors of the canonical book
Divinely inspired epistle
Philippines
Start by showing their world view

Who are they?
Paul and Timothy
By their self admission are
Servants of Christ Jesus
They are proud of their servant status

Proud to have a master
Not being one's own person
Lacking independence
Proclaiming belonging to another's rule
That's what Paul and Timothy did

Such attitude of servanthood
Flies against the face of modern concept of
Democracy
When was the last time that you heard someone refer to himself
As the servant of Christ Jesus?

Paul and Timothy are proclaiming allegiance to Christ
In their admission of oath of fidelity to their master
That was their identity marker
Owned by Christ
To do His work

These servants of Christ were servants of the Holy One
The second person in the Trinity
Who became incarnate
Took on human flesh
To die for the sins of those who believe in Him

These servants of the Holy One
Addressed others who have put themselves
Under the submission of the headship of Christ Jesus
The one and only true God
Who redeems his followers through his own sacrificial death

Those who believe in Christ Jesus
The Holy One
Are sanctified in His blood
His death that was done as propitiation
For those who put their faith in Him

Being a Christian
Is not creating a democratic state
Christianity has one Lord and one God
The Triune God of the Bible
And His authority is all encompassing

Whatever the Triune God decides goes
God's ideal government for his people
Is not democracy
But monarchy with Christ as King and Lord
How difficult it is for those in Democracy to understand God's Kingdom

So foreign
So strange
Seeming so unfair
We have been brainwashed with democratic ideals
And they impede the way we understand God's plan for His people,
    the Christians

The holy ones
Saints of Christ Jesus
That's what Christians are
And it is to them that Paul and Timothy address their letter
Those who have acknowledged Jesus Christ as the master

To have Christ Jesus as Lord
Master
Changes the world view
It changes the way one perceives herself
The way one perceives her place in the world

Who are you?
How do you perceive others?
What descriptive title is used to describe yourself to others?
This is affected by how you perceive Jesus Christ
And your relationship to Him

Is Jesus Christ your master?
Or is your concept of democracy
Militantly opposed to submitting to the Kingdom of Christ
With Christ as King?
What is your *Weltanshauung*?

"The Source Of Peace"
Philippians 1:2

Paul and Timothy send greetings to fellow Christians
Grace and peace to you from God our Father
And the Lord Jesus Christ
Two persons in the Trinity
A doctrine grounded in the Bible

Paul and Timothy do not merely wish
That Paul and Timothy enjoy grace and peace
But that they are reminded that
They receive them as blessing from the Triune God
Even in their greeting, the servants of Christ teach

It is not peace
As the world defines it
That Christians seek
If Christians define peace in the same way the world defines it
Then, there is something seriously wrong

Jesus of Nazareth said
That he came to divide
Not to unite
Christ is the Prince of Peace
But in spiritual terms

Just as Jesus did not come to bring political peace
Christians must not stand primarily for political peace
For the sake of Truth
Wars must be fought
Also for justice

This is implicit in the greeting
May grace and peace be
From God our Father
And the Lord Jesus Christ
The source of true grace and peace

It is not peace
As the world defines it
That Christians seek
And hope for
But peace from Christ

H.C. Kim

Christians by definition
Are in Christ
And focus on Christ
Jesus is the reference point
The world does not even compare

True Christians
Will fight for true peace
And will not be satisfied by political peace
That promotes injustice
Christ alone is the source of true peace

"To Be Remembered With Thanksgiving"
Philippians 1:3

I thank my God
Every time I remember you
So write the servants of Christ
Can other Christians say such things about you?

It is hard to be the reason for other's thanksgiving to God
Because humans beings fail
To err is to be human
So goes the saying

To be an encouragement to other Christians
To the extent that they thank God on account of you
When they pray
Is a difficult thing to be

It must sure be an evidence
Of the stamp of Christ in their lives
How else could they be such a great source of joy
For the ones who are sharing the Gospel

In the midst of suffering
The servants of Christ
Thanked God for the fellow believers
Who encouraged

Today
There is just too much condemnation
Of those who are in Christ
Trying to spread the True Gospel

There must be more teamwork
In the work to uphold the correct doctrine
To advance the Kingdom of Christ on earth
It is like a mustard seed that will grow

To be remembered with thanksgiving
Is something that Christians must think about
To be a reason for other Christians rejoicing
Even in the midst of their suffering for the Gospel

"Partnership In The Gospel"
Philippians 1:4-5

To be a partner
In a law firm means sharing in the firm's destiny
Profits will be shared
And loses will reflect personally on the partners

To be a partner
In marriage
Means sharing the future
As one

To be a partner
In a tennis game
Is being there to complement the teammate
To cover the weak spots

Partners are important
Not only from a functional standpoint
But as a morale support
This is the case with Gospel work as well

Paul thanks God for the partners in the Gospel
That he has among the Christians in Philippi
They were there from day one
So Paul always prays with joy when he prays for them

What is the Gospel?
The truth that Jesus Christ is God
That faith in Christ is what saves
And it was the plan of God prophesied in the Old Testament

The Christians in Philippi were partners in this Gospel
Paul in the midst of his suffering as a minister of the Gospel
Had a source of joy
The brothers and sisters in Christ in Philippi

"Completion"
Philippians 1:6

Starting work
Continuing in work
One looks towards
Fruitful conclusion
The laborer wants to see the fruits of his labor

Often
One doubts if there will be a successful end
To all the toil
There is worry
Emotional investment

Working hard for the Gospel of Jesus Christ
St. Paul wanted to bear fruit
Through his ministry
He was concerned with good result
That the Gospel work will end in joy

In the midst of exerting effort
For the Gospel
Desiring successful Christian walk
For his fellow Christian brothers and sisters
Paul prayed

And the Apostle had
Faith
Confidence in the providential work of Christ
That the good work He began
He will bring to good completion

Not only would Christ be faithful
In the Gospel work
Guiding it
In Paul's life time
But until the day of Christ Jesus

Yes, Christ Jesus is coming back
In His full glory
On that day the dead will rise to resurrection
To receive eternal life or eternal punishment
That is the day of Christ Jesus

This is why St. Paul could work for the Gospel
Without fear
Because he knew that whatever happens to him
The work of the Gospel to which he dedicated his life
Will be successful

It did not depend on his personal success
Even if he were killed working for the Gospel
It would not be a failure
For God is in control
And He will see the Gospel work to fruitful conclusion

Faith in God
Demands faith in His providence
Trusting in Christ
Means acknowledging that He is the Lord
Creator of the World

St. Paul trusted in the Triune God of the Bible
Who created the World
Who guides His creation
Who promises the Day of Judgment
When Christ Jesus returns in His full glory

"Defending And Confirming The Gospel"
Philippians 1:7-8

The Gospel
What comes to mind when you hear this word?
Often it is forgotten
That it is something to be
Defended and confirmed

But St. Paul describes his ministry
As defending and confirming the Gospel
Of course
The idea of sharing the love of Christ is implicit
But what is stated is stated

Today
Too many Christians forget
That it is a vital work of Christianity and all Christians
To defend the Gospel
Christian apologetics is important

How many Christian seminaries
Offer good courses on the defense of Christianity?
The history of how Christians defended Christianity
And how Christians should defend the Gospel
Today

Sometimes, you just have to wonder
If Christian leaders are capable of defending the Gospel
In the modern political and social contexts
They have lost the spirit of Paul
Who defended the Gospel, risking his life in the process

Why doesn't anybody talk about defending the Gospel anymore?
How many sermons are preached on the need to spread the Gospel?
Defending the truth of the Gospel
Is important
That is crucial to Christian work

How does the New Testament describe Christian work?
It is important to go back to the root of Christianity
People who say that they respect the Bible
Should act like they do
What makes Christianity what it is?

Who attacks the Gospel?
Against whom should Christian ministers defend the Gospel of Christ?
Every Christian must first acknowledge that Christianity must be defended
The Church as a family of Christ
Must work to defend the Gospel together

Sharing in the work of Christ
Means encouraging defense of the Gospel
In friendly as well as hostile settings
St. Paul was in chains
In prison because of his work to defend the Gospel

There is a recognized hostility to the Christian Gospel in the Bible
It was not all in St. Paul's head
Brothers and sisters in Christ in Philippi recognized this as well
And they participated in the Gospel work
To defend and confirm the Gospel of Christ

Why don't Christian leaders actively acknowledge
Hostility to Christianity in today's society
Christianity must be defended and confirmed
It is an integral work of Christian ministry
Of every Christian church in the world

St. Paul can honestly say that
The Christians in Philippi were an encouragement to his work
Even when he is in jail for Christ
Because they acknowledged and supported the need to defend the Gospel
At all cost

Are you a Christian
Like those praised by St. Paul?
Can Christian leaders who suffer for the Gospel Truth
Say that you are an encouragement to them
As they suffer, trying to defend the Gospel?

"Love Abounding Knowledge"
Philippians 1:9-11

Christian doctrine is important
Because it is founded on the Bible
Knowledge is crucial
So is depth of insight

That is why St. Paul prays
For love abounding in knowledge
Christian love is based on
The teachings of the Bible

But why?
Why is it important that love abounds in knowledge?
Because Christian love is to produce something concrete
First, to discern what is best

What is best for the work of the Gospel
For love of Christ
Was the love shown through the work on the cross
So sharing of Christ's love is integrally related to the Gospel work

Caring about Christian ministry was indeed
A primary concern of St. Paul
And he wanted it to be a central concern of
His brothers and sisters in Christ

Second, to be pure and blameless until the day of Christ
To live in imitation of the Holy Trinity
For humans were created in the image of the Triune God
And salvation through Christ provides a process of restoration of that image

The fall in the Garden of Eden
Through Adam and Eve
Caused corruption of all creation
Death did enter the world through the Fall

But salvation through faith in Christ Jesus
Provides a process of restoration
Reconciliation
Of the saved creature to the Creator

Walking on the road of sanctification
The regenerate Christian will fail and sin
But all the while he will walk towards the point of glorification
Which will be complete upon the return of Christ in the Second Coming

The sanctification process is a difficult process
When we struggle to be more like the Triune God
For we were created in His image
To be blameless is our goal

But the fruit of righteousness is a gift of God
For it comes through Jesus Christ
All our good deeds after being saved
Must be seen as proceeding from the grace of Christ

So, even in our righteous living
We cannot take the credit
And glorify ourselves
Only Christ deserves the glory

To the glory and praise of God
St. Paul emphasizes
God is the Creator
Sustainer

As the first question of the Westminster Shorter Catechism
Emphasizes
The main purpose of human existence is
To glorify the Triune God and enjoy Him forever

This doctrinal point
As one can see
Is firmly rooted in the Bible
God deserves the glory for everything

The whole purpose of love
Abounding in knowledge
Is ultimately to glorify God
And enjoy Him forever

"To Advance The Gospel"
Philippians 1:12

What is St. Paul's strategic purpose?
Clearly
To advance the Gospel
That is his chief concern

Absolutely obsessed
That's what St. Paul was
To advance the interests of the Gospel message
Not his own interests

Paul did not care if he suffered personally
Or went without comforts that others enjoyed
Even psychological torment would be endured
All for the sake of the Gospel

Total dedication to what Jesus taught
And His redemptive work on the Cross
The message that Jesus is the only way to salvation
That was the primary concern for St. Paul

Thus, Paul emphasizes
That what happened to him
Has advanced the Gospel
He wants to make sure that fellow Christians know this

If Paul were asked
What was his heart's desire?
He would surely have answered
To advance the Gospel

It did not matter
What condition he was in
What suffering he had to endure
As long as the Gospel is advanced

Being imprisoned for advancing the Gospel
Would be a source of thanksgiving
For the Christian dedicated to the Gospel
This was the attitude of St. Paul

"I Am In Chains For Christ"
Philippians 1:13

To be in chains
Is a horrible thing
You are deprived of liberty
And freedom

To be shackled
Sends a message
He is a criminal
Who is in chains

Communist governments
Put thinkers and writers in chains
In order to assassinate their character
So that their message would fall on deaf ears

Who would listen to one in chains?
The one who is humiliated and degraded
Can't possibly be a leader
People would despise them like criminals

Perhaps, the power thinks thus?
Jesus was put into chains
And humiliated
Suffered a criminal's death

Did public humiliation
And the wrongful application of law
Abrogate the message of Christ Jesus?
Certainly not!

As in the case of Jesus
His message stood dignified
In the midst of his apparent infamy
And public humiliation

As Jesus' naked body hung there
On the cross next to real criminals
His humiliating nakedness visible to the world
Did not hide the honor of his teaching

In the same way
St. Paul was certain
That he being in chains
Would accomplish the opposite of what his persecutors wanted

The shackles that bound St. Paul
Were on account of his dedication to Christ
St. Paul knew it
And others did, too

Even the guards who put St. Paul in chains
Knew that St. Paul did not do anything wrong
It was for Christ that he was in prison
This was also the case with the guards watching Jesus

St. Paul does not mind being in chains
As long as the Gospel is advanced
The message of the Gospel is beautiful
Even if the bearer of the Gospel is in ugly and oppressive chains

As much as power hungry authority
Wants to block the Gospel truth
It will spread because of the innate truth of its message
There is power in the Word

Perhaps, this provides how God operates in the world
In His divine providence?
Although many dissenters were persecuted by Communist regimes
Put in chains

Their message
Cry for freedom
Won
People were attracted to the message

This is a general grace reflection
Of the reality
Of special grace
Gospel truth stands up to oppression

As in the case of special grace
Jesus' message overcoming chains and the Cross
St. Paul's message standing firm in the midst of imprisonment
The Word proceeding forth

It was the case with general grace
In cases that did not involve the Gospel
In communist regimes where dissenters were persecuted
Their message withstood oppression

The former Czechoslovakia is a testimony to this
Other communist regimes as well
Certain social truths
Held firm in the midst of attempts to destroy the message

So, how much more true in the case of eternal Truth!
The Gospel message will not be destroyed by attempts at
Character assassination of the bearers of the message
Nor the Truth destroyed by force of arms

St. Paul knew that he was in chains for Christ
Even the guards watching him day and night knew
And others as well
The message of the Gospel actually spread through this reality

"Because Of My Chains"
Philippians 1:14

As a result of the Fall
The creation is reluctant to give honor to God
Which is due Him
The Creator

Sin entered the world
Through Adam and Eve
And His creatures
Are afraid to praise Him

This explains why we Christians are
Timid
Shy
Embarrassed

To share the message of the Gospel with others
There is an inherent fallen nature
That militates against the
Desire to share the Gospel message with others

Even the regenerate
Those who have personally received salvation
Through the death and resurrection of Christ
Are loath to share the Gospel message from which they have benefited

It is the fall that encourages the sinful desire not to proclaim
The Gospel
But our proactive sinful nature
Also discourages proclamation of the honor of the Triune God

Even when we are justified
That is, born again in Christ,
We are not perfect
Carnal flesh will persist until the coming of Jesus Christ

Until we have resurrected
Perfect bodies at the Second Coming
Our sinful bodies will militate against proclaiming Christ as King
Even if we are born again

That was the case in Paul's time
Christians were afraid to share the Gospel
That is the case today
It is easier to keep one's mouth shut in public

St. Paul tells
It was because he was in chains
That fellow Christians actually were encouraged to overcome
Their fear about talking about Christ in public

Boy, did the oppressive power miscalculate things!
They wanted to shut St. Paul up
So they put him in chains
But not only did St. Paul not shut up

Other Christians who were previously afraid
To talk about Christ to others
To non-Christians
Now they gained fearlessness to talk about Christ

It was like Murphy's Law in action
An example of a policy miss
Advancing history towards the opposite direction
There are a lot of examples like this in human history

St. Paul testified
Because of my chains
Because of my chains
Because of my chains

"Motives Do Not Matter"
Philippians 1:15

Today's Christian ethicists are often not very Christian
They have become academics
Not living ethicists
What makes a Christian ethicist precisely that?

A Christian ethicist is bound by the Christian text
Without the standardized Christian text
An ethicist cannot be called a Christian ethicist
The adjective is qualified by the New Testament perspective

Thus, when a scholar says that motives are more important than action
Or even if motives have to be good
Then, he is not speaking out of the Christian perspective
Christianity does not say if the motive is bad then action should not be
    taken

Nowhere is this brought out more clearly
Than in the proselytism program of the New Testament
When Jesus' disciples came and complained
There were those who were healing and preaching in Jesus' name

Jesus of Nazareth did not say
That it is wrong that those who were not directly linked
To Jesus and his 12 disciples
Should preach the Gospel in Jesus' name

Jesus affirmed that it was good that they healed and preached in His name
Jesus did not question their motives
It did not matter
Even if their motives were bad or sinful

The important issue for Christ
Was that the Gospel is preached in His name
A kingdom divided against itself will not stand
So Jesus' followers are to stand together against enemies of Christ

To proselytize Jews
That's what Jesus did
And those who were healing and preaching in Jesus' name did
As long as the Kingdom of Christ is advanced, motives do not matter

It is this Christian ethics
That St. Paul holds onto and teaches
To the Christians in Philippi
Converting others to Christianity is what is important

It does not matter if the motive is bad
Or sinful
Envy is sin, no?
Rivalry is bad, no?

St. Paul
Like Jesus Christ
Does not care about motives
It doesn't matter if it is out a good motive or a sinful one

What is important to St. Paul
Is that Jews and Gentiles alike are converted into Christianity
Evil motives are okay
Just as long as the Kingdom of Christ is advanced

This is Christian ethics
Christian ethics does not demand that motives be pure
It demands that the Kingdom of Christ be advanced
Christian ethics is by definition Christ-centered

That is why God can do no wrong
God can commit genocide and He did
And that is perfectly ethical in Christian ethics
God is by definition righteous

God commits genocide
He is good
God sends rain onto a draught laden land
He is good

God sets ethics
Christian ethics is Christ-centered
In Paul's Christian ethics
Motives are subjugated under proselytism

The *raison d'être* of Christianity is proselytism
There is no purpose for Christianity
But to convert non-Christian
This is nowhere more evident than in the Great Commission

For this central focus of Christianity
Early Christians were persecuted and killed
They were seen as a threat by non-Christians
They held onto Christian ethics

Christian ethics in its fundamental basis
Is that Christianity is good and is need for all
Jews, Gentiles don't matter
Focused on this, Christian proselytism is the focus of Christian ethics

Ends do justify the means
Certainly the motives
It is better to have sinful motives and proselytize
Than have good motives and not

Christian ethics as defined by Paul
And Jesus is clear
A Christian ethicist is bound by the Christian text
If she rejects the text, than she is no Christian ethicist
And certainly her character is in doubt
For lying and misrepresenting herself
As a Christian ethicist
When she rejects the Christian text

"Those Who Preach Out Of Good Will"
Philippians 1:16

There are those with good motives
Who preach the Gospel out of good will
That St. Paul does affirm
But notice how he defines good will

Paul states that those with good will do out of love
Out of love for whom?
For St. Paul
He does not say that they do so out of love for those whom they try to
  convert

St. Paul states that good will
Good intention
Equals acknowledging that Paul is suffering for Christ
That defines good will

Is that really how we would define good will?
Good motive?
Isn't St. Paul being selfish?
Those who acknowledge him have good intentions

What is the Apostle emphasizing?
He is concerned with the Christian community being a Christian
  community
The primary import of the Christian community is to proselytize
  non-Christians
Secondary goal is to look after the Christians

Taking care of Christ-rejecting Jews
Is not what Paul cares about
He is concerned about Christians taking care of Christians
Jews who reject Christ, just like Gentiles who reject Christ, will burn
  forever in Hell

So St. Paul defines good motive
As loving him
And supporting his ministry
You might think that Paul's teaching on good motive is selfish?

Being a Christian is not being nice to others
Christians belong to Christ and fundamentally support the Kingdom of
    Christ
Christians will be resurrected unto life at Jesus' return
Jews and Gentiles who reject Christ will be resurrected to eternal
holocaust in Hell

St. Paul fundamentally defends Christian interests
He is not concerned about defending Christ-rejecting Jewish interests
Of Pagan interests
This is the ethics of Paul

"Hostile Motives"
Philippians 1:17

Hostile motives
Some Christians certainly had that
Of course
They did
All human beings are totally depraved

Total Depravity
Unconditional Election
Limited Atonement
Irresistible Grace
Perseverance of the Saints

All human beings are innately sinful
With selfish motives
In Adam, we sinned all
As the Puritans have taught
And the Bible affirms

It doesn't matter if you are a born-again Christian
You are sinful with sinful desires
This will not change
Until Jesus Christ comes back
And give us resurrected, incorruptible bodies

Christians have selfish motives
Just like non-Christians
Christians commit sin
Just like non-Christians
The difference is that Christians are adopted into the family of Christ

The difference is that Christians go to Heaven
Non-Christians go to Hell
Those who believe in Christ are justified by Christ's righteousness
Not their own
Faith is a gift of God

So
You certainly will have Christians
Preaching Christ out of evil motives
Selfish ambition
Hostile intent

St. Paul even affirms that there were Christians
Who were preaching the Gospel
While trying to cause problems for Paul
When he was in prison
These Christians wanted to kick St. Paul when he was down

What does the Apostle say?
That they should stop in their work for the Gospel
Because their intentions were evil?
They were interested in doing Paul harm
When he was suffering

No
Paul does not say that
Because their intentions were sinful
They should stop their proselytism efforts
Certainly not

Paul innately recognizes that Christians are sinful
I do what I do not want to do
I do not do what I want to do
This is the testimony of the regenerate Paul
He understands that Christians are still in the sinful world

Christians will invariably act out of sinful intention
Some times
Most times
That does not matter
What is important is that Christ is preached

Proselytism is what is important in Paul's writing
In this, Paul follows Jesus of Nazareth
The Gospel must be preached
And Jews and Gentiles must be converted
This is the fundamental reason why Christianity exists

It is okay to have sinful, evil motives
Even if you are trying to do other Christians harm
As long as
You are preaching the Gospel as represented in the Bible
This is Christian ethics

All else is subjugated under the interests of Christ
Christ must be preached
Christ must be advanced
In the midst of all human sin and faults and evil motives
Christian proselytism efforts must not end

"I Rejoice"
Philippians 1:18

Not only is it okay
And good
That Christ is preached
By those who have sinful motives
Even wanting to do harm to Paul when he is in chains

St. Paul says
That he will rejoice
Not only that
He will continue to rejoice
That the Gospel is being preached

For Paul
What is important is that Jews and Gentiles are converted to Christianity
Even sinful motives in evangelism are good
As long as the message of the cross is advanced
It wasn't about Paul, it was about Christ

It wasn't about the Jews
It wasn't about the Gentiles
It wasn't about good motives
It wasn't about evil motives
It was all about Christ

St. Paul will rejoice
As long as the Gospel is preached
The Kingdom of Christ is advanced
Even by those who want to do him personal harm
That doesn't matter

But implicitly Paul rejects anyone who has good motives
Who does not preach the Gospel
Who does not have Christ's interest at the center
Good motives is certainly evil
When it opposes Christian proselytism

The focus of Christianity is Christ
And Christ crucified
Resurrected from the dead
It is the demand that every Christian proselytize
Even if with evil motives

So don't condemn TV evangelists
To condemn them when they are preaching the true Gospel
Is condemning Christian ethics as set out by St. Paul
Even if they are making millions of dollars and that is their primary goal
As long as they are preaching the Gospel, then their work is good

Sinful motives do not abrogate their work
As long as the Gospel is preached
Human beings are sinful
Will be sinful even after salvation
Until Christ comes back and gives perfect bodies

So don't fuss about motives
But do emphasize that Christ must be preached
Why?
Because Jesus does
St. Paul follows Jesus in this matter

"My Deliverance"
Philippians 1:19

St. Paul was suffering
Yes, suffering for preaching the Gospel
Standing up for the Truth always has its price
Because the earth is under sin
Since the Fall of Adam and Eve

It is natural in the sinful state
To reject Christ as King
And to reject Christian proselytism as good
This is the fundamental principle of the fallen humanity
Even our enlightenment is a sinful one

Sin begets sin
Sinful nature begets sinful ethics
Christ will be missed
Christian proselytism will be rejected
Fundamentally opposing the principles of Christ

So, of course
St. Paul suffered
Sin was everywhere
He knew because he as a Jew
Had been active in persecuting Christians before his conversion

Jewish authorities sanctioned persecution of Christians
Torturing of Christians
Killing of Christians
Because the message that Jesus is God was offensive to them
The Jews hated Christians

So, St. Paul knew
The reality
He was on the other side before
The grace of Christ
Redeemed him

Now, he was suffering for the Gospel
For preaching Christ
And saying that Christian proselytism is important
Perhaps he preached that Jews are the children of devil
The way Jesus preached

Maybe Paul told the Pagans that their gods are lifeless
That there is only life in Christ Jesus
The only way
The Truth and the Light
No one comes to the Father except through Christ

Such a message probably sounded uneducated to lofty Graeco-Roman
     philosophers
Such a narrow message offended the enlightened universalists in the
     Hellenistic world
Christians must have seemed narrow-minded and stupid to the Pagans
Christians roused hatred in the hearts of Jews who said there is no God
     besides the Jewish God
After all, Jews killed Christ because He claimed to be God

St. Paul stood as a Christian
In the midst of self-proclaimed superior knowledge of the Graeco-
Romans
The religiosity of the Jews
Christ-haters
Killers of Christians

Yes, it is all understandable why Paul was in chains
He preached that Jesus was the only way
That no one comes to the Father except through Christ
But he knew that this was the Truth
And the Truth shall set him free

Jesus' message was his salvation
So, St. Paul could say confidently
That his imprisonment on earth would turn out for his salvation
What we see is not the ultimate reality
The ultimate reality is in Christ, so is true freedom

"Whether By Life Or By Death"
Philippians 1:20

St. Paul is concerned about one thing
And one thing only
That Jesus Christ is proclaimed
As the only way to salvation
That He is God

He is worried about one thing
His human weakness
St. Paul is afraid that he will be ashamed
That he would lose courage
To proclaim the Truth

To be afraid
To have fear
How many Christians have this today?
Even theologians are afraid
To speak

They remain silent
Even if they personally believe that Jesus is God
Even when they have experienced personal salvation in Christ
Some theologians are ashamed
What if others will not think me intellectual enough?

Even when Christ is the most important thing in their lives
That their lives do not have meaning without Christ
Some theologians are ashamed of Christ
And deny Christ
Keeping their mouth shut

They don't want to speak up and say
Jesus Christ is God
He is the only way to salvation
And certainly they don't want to put that in print
What if people see me narrow minded?

This is the fear
Angst
That St. Paul had
That he would become ashamed of the Gospel
That had set him free

To lose courage is easy
Some could threaten with pain and torture
Some cold threaten to take away your life
Some could take away your livelihood
And leave you destitute, alone, a living dead

To be brave is hard
Because it means standing up against the majority
Who wants to hear that Jesus Christ is God?
Saying that everyone is right is easier than saying Christ is right
At the exclusion of everyone else

Sure
Attacks could come
They probably will come
So even in your deep heart
You believe that Jesus is God

It takes tremendous courage to speak up
And how many theologians will
Probably not many
It's just too difficult
And today's theologians have too much to lose by propagating the Gospel

No wonder the churches are shrinking
Theologians who are supposed to be defending the Gospel
Have lost heart and courage
That is what St. Paul feared
That he would be timid at the wrong thing

It is easy to speak up
On issues that everyone wants to hear
There is no personal sacrifice
Or honor in that
It is hard when you stand up for the Truth even when it means giving
    up your all

Today's theologians
Are only a shell of what Christian theologians were in the past
When they risked their lives for Christ
Thomas Cranmer was burned at the stake
Martin Luther had to hide out for years

49

To be a theologian in the past
Almost meant being ready to risk your life
It wasn't an arm chair theology exercise
But today
Theologians have no guts

Instead of defending Christ
And the Christian church
Christian theologians are jumping backwards and forwards
To defend Jewish interest
At the expense of Christ and Christ's Kingdom

Instead of proclaiming the Gospel of Christ
Today's theologians are proclaiming
Political Correctness
In a truly pagan fashion
It existed among Graeco-Roman pagans

Today's theologians do not know what it means to be Christian theologians
To stand up for Christ
To defend the truth in the Gospel of Christ
To risk one's life for Christ who has saved them
No wonder theologians are losing respect even among the enemies of Christ

How many theologians can shout with St. Paul
Whether by life or by death
May Christ be exalted through my life
My work
My defense of the Gospel of Christ

This explains the sad state of the church
Theologians who are not doing their God-demanded responsibility
They are running around
Trying to serve their master
Political Correctness

"For To Me"
Philippians 1:21

The Gospel has not lost its power
It is the Christian theologian who has abandoned the Gospel
There is power in the Holy Spirit
It is the Christian theologian who does not know what that power is
God still works in His creation
It is the Christian theologian who has not experienced God's work

How many so-called Christian theologians will be burning forever in Hell?
Why are they wasting time doing Christian theology if they don't want
    to defend Christ?
Meaningless, meaningless
All those hours spent in theology libraries
Reading great human minds
In the end these theologians will be burning in Hell, forever

If they do not care about Christ
Why don't they just study something else?
There are so many other disciplines that can benefit humankind
The purpose of theology is not to benefit humankind
It is to defend Christ
To strengthen the Christian church

If you want to do good for the society apart from Christ
Become a doctor and heal the sick
Both Christians and non-Christians need treatment on this earth
Even if Christians will be in Heaven forever
And non-Christians will experience eternal death in Hell
If you don't care about the afterlife, then do "good" on this earth before
    going to Hell

You could add to God's general grace
Even if you might never taste God's special grace
Theology apart from Christ is meaningless
So don't waste your time studying it if you want to do it apart from Christ
There are many interesting things out there
That benefit humanity

Christian theology is for defending Christ and the Christian church
The role of the Christian theologian is to defend Christ and the Christian
    church
Even if it means dying for it
Even if it means suffering for it
Christianity must be defended from its enemies
Learn from the Crusades

To defend the Gospel
That is important
Fight with the Word of God as if with the sharpest blade
Cut through enemies of the Gospel with the Bible
As the Crusade swords took the life out of the enemies of Christ
Stand proud on the Word of God with the full armor of Christ

For to me
St. Paul states
To live is Christ
To die is gain
The Christian theologian must learn from St. Paul's attitude
The Christian theologian exists to defend the Gospel of Jesus Christ

"Fruitful Labor"
Philippians 1:22

It almost sounds like Paul is contemplating suicide
Doesn't it
What shall I choose?
To go on living in the body or not
But, of course, Paul wasn't contemplating suicide

It wasn't the same kind of monologue as
"To be or not to be, that is the question"
Paul innately understood that life belongs to God
God is sovereign and in control
St. Paul was not contemplating suicide

Paul knew, however
That there were two possibilities for him
He can go on living
Even if it means in chains and in suffering
Or he will be killed for the Gospel that he preaches

St. Paul is contemplating
What he would prefer
While recognizing God's implicit sovereignty
One option is to go on living in the body
He knows that this would mean fruitful labor for him

St. Paul knows that he was called to be a Christian theologian
To minister to Christ's people
To defend the Truth
He recognized Christ's call
And was ready to toil for Christ if he continued to live

What an attitude!
To live means to work for Christ
To do all that one could to advance Christ
Use strategy and effective defense
To protect the Christian Gospel

How many theologians have concerns such as this, today?
How many Christian ministers care about this?
How many individual Christians think about this?
To be a Christian is to defend Christ and proclaim His Gospel

The life we live should be structured around this central focus of
Christianity

St. Paul understood
And he wanted to relay the central tenet of Christianity
To the Christians in Philippi
What does it mean to be a Christian theologian?
What does it mean to be a Christian?

"To Be With Christ"
Philippians 1:23

To be with Christ
The desire to be united with the Savior
Is the desire of every Christian
For the Christian belongs
Heart and soul to Him

It is not escapism
The true Christian does not want to run away
From the problems of this world
It is not a negative inclination
But a positive force drawing the Christian

It is better by far
To depart
And be united with Christ
A Christian must recognize this
For Christ is the center of a Christian's life

For what is there in this world
That is more attractive
More desirable
Than being united with the Savior God
Who redeemed us from the Cross?

A born-again Christian
Is
Necessarily
Looking towards Christ
To eternal life with Him

St. Paul
Like all the Catholic saints
Christian martyrs
Desired to be with Christ
That was the first choice

It is a question of the primary
Reference point
Being Christ-centered
What is your desire?
Where is your belonging?

"For You, I remain"
Philippians 1:24

Suffering Paul
The saint
Who was cast into jail
By governing authorities
Pursued to the point of death by Jews
Whom he had abandoned at conversion

He wanted to be with Christ
To be closer to Jesus
That was his desire
The longing in his heart
Oh, how he wished to be with
Jesus the Savior God

But why?
Why then did St. Paul desire to remain
To stay on this earth
And endure suffering and humiliation?
Oh, why?
Why?

It was for fellow Christians
In Philippi
It was for their sake that St. Paul
Mustered
Courage to remain
Desire to be there for them

Such is Christian love
It is not that you do what you want to do
But what is needed for other Christians
The Christian motive
Is Christ-centered
Loving other Christians is a part of that

For what is the Church?
It is the body of Christ
Loving the Church
Is loving Christ
A true Christian is
Church-centered

For the integrity of the Church
To protect the Church
The body of Christ
Christians must be willing
Even to give up his life
The Church is that important

It is for believers
The body of Christ
The Christian Church
That St. Paul
Remains
Despite the suffering

St. Paul shows us
Two thousand years later
The right attitude
Of being a Christian
What it means to love
In the Christian sense

"The Conviction"
Philippians 1:25

Paul is convinced
Perhaps like he never was before
That he needed to be there
To guard the faith
Of fellow Christians

St. Paul was willing
To suffer
Be thrown into jail
Endure
Humiliation

Conviction
Selfless in nature
Surely
Imitation of Christ
Who suffered

Yes
Christ died on the Cross
Not because he committed any sin
Christ is God
Who wanted to save His people

In self-giving sacrifice
Jesus gave up his life
To give you and me
Eternal life
Redeeming us from Hell

It is this spirit
That St. Paul has
The apostle
Wanted to be there
For them

Like Christ
St. Paul was willing to
Suffer
Even die
For the people of Christ

St. Paul was determined
Through his conviction in Christ
To encourage the progress of fellow Christians
So that they might experience
Joy in Christ

To be like Jesus
That was the desire of St. Paul
To encourage Christians
That was his heartfelt wish
For Paul knew that he himself was bought with Christ's blood

"Joy To Go Around"
Philippians 1:26

Spread it around
Like jam
Tasty and savory
All over the bread
Cover it completely

Like honey overflowing
Let the sweetness fill the jar
Attracting bees
From miles around
Who could stay away from such a taste

Like chocolate
That melts in the mouth
Pleasant sensations staying
Long afterwards
Let it dominate

Oh!
Joy in Christ
Something to desire
Long after
Hold onto

St. Paul experienced
Joy in Christ
And he wanted his fellow
Christian believers
To experience this joy

It's joy that abounds
Even in the midst of suffering
Filled with optimism
And hope
That is Christian joy

Deeply in the heart of the Christian
There is trust in Christ
Despite all the suffering
Sadness
Misfortune

The Christian gets
Strength
From Christ
The source of joy
Unfettered

St. Paul wanted to add to
Christian joy
By his presence and encouragement
Christ is everything
Without Him there is no joy

The joy of
St. Paul was
Of course
Joy in Christ
The source of true joy

It's like joy
Squared
It grows exponentially
No one could ever get bored with it
Christian joy to go around

"Contending As One Man"
Philippians 1:27

It's a strategy
Like in a football game
Players huddled together
To plan
To execute it
To win

Christian life
Is like one big
Game
To win souls for Christ
To protect the honor of Christ
It requires good strategy

Offense
Winning souls for Christ
One born again Christian
One point
Play good offense
And the game could be won

Defense
You can't ignore it
You can't win a game with just
Good offensive
Being offensive is important
But it has to go hand-in-hand with good defensive

Like a faithful defensive linebacker
You have to protect
With your body
Soul
Your all
To win

Christ's honor has to be protected
Use your creativity
Education
Personal experiences
Talents
Everything to win the game

Think of the Christian life as a game
And play as if you were one player
The team should be united
With the same goal
Win the game!
Win the game!

St. Paul teaches
Conduct yourself in a manner worthy of the Gospel
Why?
The answer lies in the second half of the verse
Philippians chapter one
Verse twenty-seven

Contending as one man
For the faith of the Gospel
It is a strategy with a purpose
You act in order to win
Win souls for Christ
Defend the honor of Christ

Christianity is a
Game
Rules are set by Christ
Jesus the Judge
Every Christian plays to win
Points for Christ and His Kingdom

"Like A Good Coach"
Philippians 1:28

St. Paul
Call him
"Coach"
Paul the Coach
Directs

Hey, don't be a wuss!
Don't be afraid
Stand tall, man
Defense!!
Offense, do your job!

St. Paul wants the Christians to win
He knows that the other team
Those anti-Christians
Will play hard
They also will play with all they have got

Of course
They are playing for the Evil One
Even if they do not know that he owns the team
But Christians know
They have inside information

Is that all you've got?
Give it your all!
Don't you know who you are playing for?
You could almost hear St. Paul's voice
That's a good coach for you

Paul the Coach
Anticipates
What the other team will do
They will use scare tactics
They will try to put you down

St. Paul
The good coach
Encourages
Do not be frightened
In any way

There will be those who oppose you
They will try to make you lose
Don't let them
Intimidate
Put one over you

Paul assures
And he most certainly believed it
He believed in his fellow Christians
The players for Christ
They played for the right team

St. Paul says in no unclear terms
They will be destroyed
Those anti-Christians who play against our team
But you
Christ's team will be saved

"Embrace Pain"
Philippians 1:29-30

Pain is good!
That is the philosophy here
To be a Christian
Means
Embracing pain

No pain, no gain
You could say that
Christians will suffer
For the world is under sin
And will reject those who stand for the truth

Suffering for Christ
Certainly
Is portrayed as an honor
In the book of Philippians
I am suffering for Christ, says Paul

Believing in Christ
Is not the only gift that you received from God
But the privilege to suffer for Christ
That is a gift of God as well
Suffering for Christ is good

Theodicy
The idea that God might not be just
If He lets the righteous suffer
Doesn't approach the question
From a Biblical perspective

Of course
By the world's standards
Suffering is bad
Period
Enjoy the world!

But the Bible is different
God's Word encourages
Standing up for Christ
Living for Jesus
Suffering with joy for the Lord Savior

Yes
Salvation in Jesus Christ is a gift of God
But
Suffering for the sake of Christ
Is a great gift of God as well

Christian attitude
Turns world's ideas
Upside down
Christianity is transformative
Revolutionary

"One In Spirit And Purpose"
Philippians 2:1-2

What a revolutionary idea!
St. Paul is basically saying
If you have any encouragement from Christ
If Christ means anything to you
If you are born again

If the Holy Spirit has touched you
If you are filled with the Spirit of God
Endowed with the power of the Word of God
Living in the Spirit
Redeemed in Christ's blood

Then you should
Be united with fellow believers
The Christians
In one spirit and
One purpose

St. Paul values Christian unity that much
Being united in Christ
Means being united against
Those who are opposed to Christ
Identity both unites and separates

Christians are those who are in Christ
Who profess that Jesus Christ is the only Lord God
That unity necessarily marks them
As different
From those who reject Christ

What is St. Paul saying?
What is his vision of Christianity?
You could reject him and his ideas
Because you don't like them
But be honest and acknowledge his central idea

Christians are united with Christians
Christians cannot be united with those who hate Christ
Who don't recognize Jesus as the true Messiah
That's what Paul is saying
Christians should be united in Christ

Be united in same love
Same love?
Love in Christ
You silly
It's pretty obvious, no?

United in common purpose
Common purpose?
To preach Christ
And Him crucified
Paul was obsessed about Christian evangelism

After all
Why was St. Paul imprisoned
Yes
Because
Paul wanted to convert everyone to Christianity

Jews hated Him
Because Paul abandoned Judaism
Claiming it as false religion
And tried to convert every Jew to Christianity
Jews felt threatened by St. Paul

Pagans hated Him
Because Paul showed that the Pagan way
Was not the way
But Christ
The truth path

Common purpose?
What was Paul's purpose?
To convert everyone to Christianity
That was the ultimate purpose
That's what Paul wanted Christians at Philippi to do

Unite
To convert others
Proselytize
Jews
Pagans

The Christian Spirit

If St. Paul were alive today
Don't you think that there would be those out to get him
Just like two thousand years ago
Jews would hate him
So would the Pagans

"Christian Humility"
Philippians 2:3

Consider others better than yourselves
St. Paul instructs the Christians in Philippi
This is not hard to do
If one believes in the Bible teaching
That all have fallen short and are sinners before God

Total Depravity
Calvinism followed the tradition of St. Augustine
Who followed the instructions of St. Paul
Who imitated Christ Jesus
The Savior God

There is beauty in the Christian tradition
And history
After all
Is not God sovereign?
Does He not guide history?

Christians cannot be but humble before God
Because we know that we are sinners
Who deserve eternal punishment in Hell
But by the blood of Christ
We are born again through the Holy Spirit

We know that we were bought at a price
So that none could boast
This attitude
Recognizing God's work of salvation in us
Keeps us humble before other human beings

We know that our righteousness
Is a gift of the Lord Jesus
Those who are not Christians
Could be given this gift by God as well
Righteousness belongs to God

A true Christian is required to be grateful to the Lord
Jesus Christ who died on our behalf
So we must not think about our own interests
But the interest of Christ
There is no room for selfish ambition

Christian humility
Is one that recognizes the work of Christ on the cross
Thanking the Lord for imputing righteousness
Giving us salvation as a gift of the Creator God
Who renews us in the blood of Christ

"The Interests Of Others"
Philippians 2:4

The interests of others?
Wow
What does this mean
It could be a thousand of things
Winning the World Cup?
That could be a wish of a soccer player in Germany

But of course
The answer is not so complicated
When we ask
What is the Biblical perspective?
What is the most important thing in the Bible?
Salvation in Christ, of course

So what are the interests of others?
That they are saved in Jesus Christ
We are to look out for other's interests
To benefit them
We have to convert them to Christ
Even if it goes against our own interests

Subjugating our own private interests
So that others might come to know Jesus Christ
That is hard to do
We might be concerned abut our reputation
Whether others will like us or not
Trying to convert others to Christianity is a difficult thing to do

But the Bible is clear
We are to look out for the interests of others
It is in other's interests
That they do not go to the eternal holocaust
In Hell
To die eternally

Even if
They don't understand that it is in their interest
To believe in Christ
And live
Isn't it important to save them
From the eternal holocaust in Hell?

Christian missions
Must be understood
As looking out for the interests of others
St. Paul was
Missionary *par excellence*
He knew what was really important

"The Attitude Of Christ"
Philippians 2:5

Christ had an attitude
He always attacked Jewish leaders
Irritating them beyond means
And so they organized to kill Him

Christ was preachy
Always saying what is necessary
And talking about God's kingdom
No one can deny that He was audacious

Although some might have seen that as pride
The Bible is clear in representing Christ as
Humble
Jesus Christ is the symbol of humility

The book of Philippians adopts the
Philosophy according to Jesus
True humility is not being embarrassed about the Gospel
Being timid about proclaiming Christ

Humility in Christian worldview
Is
Altogether different
From the worldly definition

Jesus was humble
Because while being God
He made himself into human
In the Incarnation

And He died for the sins
Of those who repent
Put their faith in Christ
And want to be born again

That is the example
Jesus was that concerned about salvation
That He willingly took on suffering
To bring salvation to non-Christians

Christians are the children of God
Not like the Jews
Whom Jesus called
Children of the Devil

But despite the fact
Christians belong to the family of Christ
Christians are to humble themselves
And bring the Gospel to non-Christians

Yes
Even to the children of the Devil
For Christ's love is transformative
Reconciling sinners to God through the blood of Christ

True Christian humility
Cannot be found
Apart from Christian witness
For to share the Gospel with others is humbling yourself

Jesus' work on the Cross
Represents His humility
The Cross is the overarching symbol of future potential
Hope in the Savior God that humbles the proud

"In Very Nature God"
Philippians 2:6

Which idiot said that
The Trinity
Is not found in the
Bible?

Make him
Eat
His own
Words!

Here it is clear
That Jesus Christ
Is in very nature
God

They are liars
Like those
Who claim that
Jews did not kill Jesus

They obviously
Have
Not
Read the Bible

What does the Text say?
Jesus Christ is God
Who took on human flesh
Jews killed Jesus

The Bible shows that
Jesus rose from the dead
Death could not bind Him
Because He is God

Jesus Christ
Is the Second Person in the Trinity
There are
Three Persons in the Godhead

God the Father
God the Son
God the Holy Spirit
Three in One

Jesus is God
In nature Christ is Divine
He is the same as God the Father
God the Holy Spirit

The Gospels portray
The Old Testament
As talking about Christ
The God

When King David worshipped God
He worshipped Jesus Christ
That's the explanation of the New Testament
Old Testament is seen through Christ

So when someone says
Jews and Christians understand the
Old Testament in the same way
He is surely mistaken

Jews are opposed to the Christian understanding
Because the Old Testament
For Christians is
Pointing to Christ Jesus

No one in Judaism
Will say the Old Testament
Shows that Jesus Christ is God
In very nature the same as the God of the Old Testament

No one in Judaism
Will say that Jesus Christ is the Savior of the World
That He is the only way to salvation
Jews are opposed to Christ

That is why Jesus called Jews
Children of the Devil
The Anti-Christ
Because Jews are Anti-Christian

Judaism is fundamentally opposed to
Christianity
Judaism's understanding of the Old Testament
Is a threat to the Christian Church

Because Judaism
Actively denies that the Old Testament talks about Christ
Jesus is God
Who became man, having both natures in the incarnate body

St. Paul was aware of the threat that Judaism
And its leaders posed to the Christian Church
That is why St. Paul was always attacking Judaism
And forms of Jewish piety

St. Paul was concerned about defending the honor of Christ
Against those who denied that Jesus is God
Jews denied that Jesus is God
Judaism still opposes the Divinity of Christ

"Being Made In Human Likeness"
Philippians 2:7

The earliest Christians knew
That Jesus was both God and man
The doctrine of incarnation exists in the earliest strata
Of Christianity

In fact
Jesus Christ proclaimed that He is God
Christ the Lord God testified that He existed before
King David in the Old Testament

God is pre-existent
Christ was in existence from before the creation
Because Jesus is God
Christ was there at the creation

When God said
Let there be light
It was Christ who spoke
For God is Trinity

Tell that to the Jews and see what they say
Judaism hates the idea that Christ is God
Christ created the world
The True God is God in Three Persons

So
It's understandable
Why the early Christians fought so much with
Judaism

The idea that Jesus is God
Christ created the world
Is offensive to Jews
Some Jews equate the Cross with the swastika

Irrational hatred
Directed at Christ
Blasphemy was the charge that Jewish leaders used
To kill Jesus Christ

The Gospel accounts show Jews
Plotting to kill Jesus at every turn
Because the idea that Jesus is God
Made them see RED

Jesus is God
In very nature God
But Jesus took upon himself human flesh
Being Incarnate

The Bible describes this as fulfillment of prophesy
Found in the Old Testament
Tell that to your Jewish friends
That the Old Testament prophecies point to Christ

Judaism is opposed to this idea
Early Christians were persecuted for
Their ideology
That Christ is God

The Christian propaganda program
To spread the Good News
Deeply offended Jewish leaders
Was not Stephen in Acts killed by Jews?

Why should this be surprising?
Judaism is opposed to the idea that Jesus is God
Judaism hated Christ and killed Christ
Judaism hated early Christians and killed some of them

Jesus proclaimed that all should convert to the
Jesus movement
Pagans, Jews,
It did not matter

Judaism reacted and killed Jesus
Paganism ignored Jesus
Christians held fast to the ideology
Christ is God who took on human flesh

"Obedient To Death"
Philippians 2:8

What does it mean?
Christ was obedient to death
Is Christ not God?
Yes, He is

So to whom was Christ obedient?
To Himself
Jesus is God
And God has a divine plan for the world

God is sovereign
God is King
Creator
Lord

God ordains history
God is the master of history
Not even one bird dropping falls without God's knowledge
God is omniscient

God as all-knowing King
Ordained what will happen in history
Even before it happened
God did reveal his plan partly to His prophets in the Old Testament

What was God's divine plan?
That He would become Incarnate
And die for the sins of those
Who believe in Him and want to be saved

Christ as the Second Person in the Trinity
Created the Divine Plan
It was to Himself and His own plan
That Christ was obedient

It is impossible for Christ as God
To oppose His own Will
So it was natural that Christ was obedient to Himself
God is consistent

Humans in contrast are not
St. Paul said
I do what I do not want to do
I do not do what I want to do

It is not so with God
God is always consistent
God plans the history
And it always comes to pass

"God Exalted Himself"
Philippians 2:9

It is totally normal
For God to exalt Himself
All exaltation to God is due
Soli Deo Gloria

So God the Father exalts
God the Son
Who in turn exalts
God the Holy Spirit

The Holy Trinity
Is perfect unity
There is a relationship of mutual exaltation of the Three Persons
In the One Godhead

Philippians
Chapter two
Verse nine
States that God exalted Jesus to the highest place

What is the highest place?
That is the place of God
Of course
This is natural

This is the way
That one of the earliest Christian hymns
Teach early Christians that
Jesus is both God and man

The doctrine of the Holy Trinity
Was central to Christianity from the very beginning
From the Jesus movement
To the theology of St. Paul

St. Paul was interested in protecting
Correct doctrine
Here is a great example of this
St. Paul was teaching about the Incarnation and Jesus' Divinity

Opposed to Judaism
Jesus is God
Jesus created the world
Christ is pre-existent

Christ of faith
Is represented in
Jesus of history
Jesus Christ is both God and man

Jesus Christ as God the Son
Stands in the same place with God the Father
God the Son
Is the Second Person in the Holy Trinity

"Every Knee Should Bow"
Philippians 2:10

Jesus is God
St. Paul is obsessed with this idea
It was for this idea
Leaders of Judaism persecuted Christians

The Gospel account describes that
The claim of Jesus to be God
Was the reason that Jews wanted to kill Jesus
Christ died on the Cross and rose again from the dead

This early Christian hymn
Proclaims that everyone should bow at the name of Jesus
It is demanding worship of Jesus
Because Jesus is God

What an offensive idea to Jews
Foolishness in the Pagan eyes
But this Christian hymn demands that everyone must bow
At the name of Jesus

Of course leaders of Judaism did not want to bow
That is why Christians were persecuted
Pagans thought that this was stupid
They had their lofty philosophy

Jesus is God
Everyone is required to bow down to Him
Some believe in Him and will go to Heaven
Some reject Him and will go to Hell

But Jesus is God
He created the world
Christ demands worship
All who don't are guilty of capital offense against God

Not believing in Christ
In God's book
Demands a punishment of eternity in Hell
It is a capital offense

H.C. Kim

God created the world
And set the rules
Who can question His demand?
He is God

All of creation must worship Christ
There is no exception
In Heaven, on earth, under the earth
That pretty much covers everything

This is the Christian Doctrine
Christ is God
Christ must be worshipped
All who don't are guilty

Jesus is the Sovereign
No worldly leader has power over Christ
If world's leaders oppose Christ
Then they must be opposed

Christianity is radical
Because it is an all-or-nothing proposition
Christ is God
Those who reject this will go to the eternal holocaust in Hell

"Every Tongue Confess"
Philippians 2:11

Every tongue must confess
That Jesus is Lord
That is the divine order
The early Christian hymn emphasizes this

It doesn't say that only Christians should confess
But everyone
Even those who are headed to Hell are required
All creation is required to confess Jesus is Lord

But there are now those who do not confess
That Jesus Christ is Lord
On this earth at least
But they will in the end

When Christ Jesus comes back to judge the quick and the dead
In his second advent
Christ will send those who believe in Him to eternal life in Heaven
Those who rejected Him to eternal death in Hell

The Christians will worship Christ in His presence in Heaven
And sing that He is LORD
Those who are burning and burning forever in Hell
Will also be forced to acknowledge that Jesus is the Lord

Christ is the King of the world
We are not talking democracy
Christianity supports Christian theocracy
That is the ideal government in heaven

So in Heaven as well as in Hell
All will be forced to recognize Jesus Christ as God
It is better to be praising Christ in Heaven
Of course

When we have the choice to accept Jesus Christ as Lord
Here on earth before our death
Or Christ' imminent return
It is better to do so now

H.C. Kim

Once Christ comes back to judge
Then there is no option
Christians will go to Heaven
Those who rejected Christ will go to Hell

"Work Out Your Salvation"
Philippians 2:12-13

Justification is once for all
When you accept Jesus Christ as your Savior God
You are saved
Born again
Hell no longer has a hold on you

But the Christian is not totally saved
In a sense
While she is on this earth
Until Christ comes back again
Christians are often persecuted

Until one dies
Or until the Second Coming of Christ
The Christian is therefore
Working out her salvation
Because this world is under the dominion of Satan

After the fall of Adam and Eve
Original sin entered the human race
Pain came into existence
People had to work and toil to live
The world was given over to Satan temporarily

In the Old Testament
Satan was given permission by God
To test Job
Satan inflicted Job with illness
Satan killed Job's loved ones

God gave Satan that much power in the world
But it is temporary
When Christ comes back again
He will cast Satan into the depth of Hell
Along with all who did not accept Jesus as their personal Savior God

Christians long for that day
When Christ returns
To judge and give out reward and punishment
Until then
Christians struggle on this earth

It is within this reality
St. Paul encourages Christians
To work out our salvation with fear and trembling
For there are those who want to destroy Christianity
And they will stop at nothing

As Jesus of Nazareth said
Fear not him who can kill the body
And he most likely was referring to Jews out to get early Christians
Jesus continued
But fear Him who can destroy the soul and cast you in Hell

St. Paul encourages Christians in Corinth
To work out their salvation with fear and trembling
They are to fear the Living God who will judge
But they are also to recognize that there is the Evil One
Who is pointing a power rifle at Christians to make them fall at all cost

Even if life is threatened
Christians are to hold fast to the Cross of Jesus Christ
After all Christ was killed
His followers are demanded to take up their cross
With willingness to die for their Savior God

Although demand is to practice one's human will
The promise is given that God is the One who is there
The Holy Spirit works in the Christian
To guide her will
To act according to God's plan

Free will
And divine plan
Are not opposed
God commands practice of free will
But mysteriously even that practice has been planned by God

God is sovereign and in control
When Job's loved ones died
It did not happen without God allowing it to happen
Satan could not carry out the death sentence without God's permission
It was all in the plan of God

Job was inflicted with illness
It was all in the divine plan of God
Satan could not have done it without God's permission
God is all-knowing
And God is all-powerful

So work out your salvation with fear and trembling
Not because you will lose your salvation
Once you are saved
You will not lose the salvation that God gave you as a gift
He is not going to take his gift away from you

But Christians are to respect God
And fear of God is an important aspect of that respect
Jesus demands fearing God
The Old Testament demands fear of God
It is the beginning of wisdom

"Hold Out The Word Of Life"
Philippians 2:14-16

Who is the Word of Life?
Jesus Christ the Lord God
What is the Word of Life?
The Bible
Which points to Jesus Christ

The goal is to hold out the Word of Life
It is not for the mere sake of not complaining
That St. Paul tells Corinthians not to complain
The whole strategic purpose of not complaining
Is to advance the Word of Life

Same goes for being blameless and pure
That is not just so that Christians could boast
About their own accomplishments
The strategy is to advance the Gospel
In good times and the bad

Shine like stars
Let the whole world know
That you are a Christian
Advance the interests of the Gospel
The Word of Life

St. Paul is working and laboring
For the same strategic goal
To advance the name of Jesus
Yes, he did love Corinthian Christians
But his primary goal is Christ-centered

St. Paul is willing to say that
He had toiled and labored for nothing
If Corinthian Christians
Fail to advance the Gospel propaganda
Effectively and strategically

It is like St. Paul is the head of a firm
Wanting results
The primary shareholder is God
It is for God's profit he labors
And he wants all the company workers to do the same

93

"A Drink Offering"
Philippians 2:17-18

Christ's sacrifice on the cross
Is celebrated in the Lord's Supper
The Eucharist
The cup represents the blood of Christ
Poured out for the salvation of those who believe in Him

Christians were accused of committing human sacrifice
By the Pagans and the Jews
Because they celebrated the Lord's Supper
Christians participate in the death of Christ
Through the symbolic reenactment of the Last Supper

It is a ritual to be sure
Filled with symbols
We drink the blood of Christ
And consume the body of Christ
Christ is the sacrificial lamb who takes away the sins of the predestined

Christ's blood was poured out like drink offering
For the sins of the redeemed
Who would have gone to eternal punishment in Hell
Otherwise
In the Lord's Supper, we participate in this mystery

St. Paul takes hold of this symbolism
Just as Christ was poured out like a drink offering
He was being poured out like a drink offering on the sacrifice
Jesus was nailed to the cross
Christ commanded His followers to take up their cross

St. Paul is basically saying that he is giving his all for them
The Christians in Philippi
In imitation of Christ
Who gave himself
On the cross

One deeply seeped in the Gospel tradition
Teachings of Christ
Biblical literary symbolism
Can easily comprehend the power
Of Paul's expression

St. Paul is offering himself for them
Freely and willingly
And with joy
St. Paul wants them to participate in the happiness
That is grounded in the Cross of Jesus

"Hope In The Lord Jesus"
Philippians 2:19

Hope
Christians have
Hope
In Christ
And it was the case with St. Paul

What was the Apostle's hope here?
That a man of God would be sent to them
The Philippian Christians
Paul valued those who were set apart for fulltime
Christian ministry

Timothy was an exceptional servant of Christ
Whom St. Paul trusted
As much as it was humanly possible to do
And St. Paul knew that
Timothy would be a spiritual encouragement for them

Even when he is wishing this
The language of St. Paul is distinctively Christian
St. Paul is hoping in Christ
For Christ is in all and be all of all things
True hope can only be found in Christ

It was hard times
Leaders of Judaism were attacking to destroy
Early Christianity
Pagans formed another front of attack
Christians were assailed from all sides

It is important to understand the difficult circumstance
In which St. Paul and early Christians found themselves
It wasn't like the comfortable situation of Christians in the USA
To be a Christian meant that it was possible to lose your job
Not only that, it was possible to die for the Christian faith

As persecutions kept coming
Hope was a difficult thing to have
But St. Paul had hope in Christ
And he encouraged other Christians
To have hope in Christ and Him alone

"Genuine Interest"
Philippians 2:20

What set Timothy apart from the rest?
In the mind of St. Paul
It was Timothy's genuine interest in
The Christians
In Philippi

St. Paul testifies
I have no one like him
It is not an easy thing to show genuine interest
It sounds easier than it is
Most are not motivated by the interests of others

You could blame the Fall for it
If Adam and Eve did not sin
And sin did not enter humanity
Perhaps
People would all be looking out for other's interest

The reality is that Adam and Eve sinned
Everyone has original sin
The world is opposed to Christ
Christians are often persecuted
To stand up for Christian interest means embracing suffering

In this climate
Timothy had strength in the Holy Spirit
To look out for the interest of the Christians in Philippi
He cared about them
Genuinely

It is not Timothy's expositional preaching that St. Paul emphasizes here
Or his holy living
Or his intelligence
Book learning
His fine personality

What sets Timothy apart from the rest is his genuine interest
For the welfare of Christians
In Philippi
He cared about them
And it was clearly visible to St. Paul

What makes a good Christian leader?
Perhaps
There is a lesson here in that regard?
Human beings are not perfect
All are sinners and Christian leaders as well

But a true Christian leader
Who would be praised by Paul
Is one who is genuinely
Concerned
About Christians

"Looking Out For Self-Interest"
Philippians 2:21

The sun rises and the sun sets
And how humans think about
The benefits that the day will bring
Self-interest

What makes the world go around?
A concern for self
What can I get out of the world?
Self-interest

The Creator looks down from above
And how foolish we must seem
Guided by what we can get out of our small world
Self-interest

Injure someone?
Never, we say
But often we do when it suits our purposes
Self-interest

Joys of capitalism
Getting ahead at other people's expense
Survival of the fittest it is, after all
Self-interest

How true it is!
What St. Paul says
Everyone looks out for his
Self-interest

World has fallen into sin
Humans are totally depraved
All seek what is good in their own eyes
Self-interest

World filled with sin
Where the righteousness of God is lacking
Will we see people looking out for other's interests?
Self-interest

"The Apple Does Not Fall Far From The Tree"
Philippians 2:22

Some say
Like father
Like son
The apple does not fall far from the tree

This was said about Timothy
By St. Paul in fact
With his father
Timothy served with Paul in the work of the Gospel

Timothy has proven himself
Like his father
As a faithful servant of the Gospel
Giving up his self-interest for that of Jesus Christ

How precious is the sweet name of Jesus
His glory is all that I seek
I bow down and pay homage to the Eternal King
Timothy might have sang in his service

How wonderful it is
When the son can share the Christian faith of his father!
What an inheritance
Richer than the greatest rubies in the world

What is the most precious thing that
Parents could bequeath to their children
Property?
Money?

No!
For Christians
The value is not in the material things
But in the spiritual

For Christ to say
Your son has the wonderful faith that you have
What a fine Christian family!
This would be the greatest blessing for a family

"First Timothy, Then Me"
Philippians 2:23-24

Trusted
Timothy was
For he was faithful
Working for the interest of Christianity

Trusting
St. Paul was
Of Timothy's work for the Christians in Philippi
He had proven himself before

The apostle was not loath
To send Timothy as his emissary
To advance the Kingdom program on his behalf
As his right hand, like an extension of his own body

The former persecutor of Christians
Now a leader of the Christian faith
Confidently worked for the Lord
Even when his own life was at stake

No one knows the tomorrow
Except the precious Lord Jesus Christ
Perhaps he sung thus
As he had faith in the omniscience and the faithfulness of God the Son

Although he could not go himself at the moment
St. Paul sent Timothy ahead of him
First Timothy
Then Paul

Fettered
Endangered
Weak
Still St. Paul thought about his Christian work

Comfortable
Not lacking
In safety
We forget the need to push on for Christ's Kingdom

How much is there to learn?
Words cannot describe
Sacrifice for Christ
St. Paul provided an example for us all

"Fellow Soldier"
Philippians 2:25

What's the deal with the military language?
It's like St. Paul sees himself at war
Here again
St. Paul uses a military term

Fellow Soldier
That's what St. Paul called Epaphroditus
A fellow warrior in a spiritual battle?
A war on behalf of the Kingdom of Christ?

Was not the Apostle aware of the implications of military language?
War kills
The soldier exists to kill
Victory depends on the destruction of the opposite side

Use of war imagery certainly
Shows St. Paul as not opposing the institution of war
War is war
Paul understood that

Horrors of war
Destruction
Loss
Desolation

Joys of war
Victory
Dominance
Enlargement of territory

Who's to say that St. Paul did not understand the implications of this?
Whenever St. Paul used war imagery
Images of wars that the Roman Empire waged
Probably were before him

The apostle knew the cost of war
He knew what it meant to lose
What it meant to win
Paul understood what being a solider entailed

In this significance
We must understand St. Paul's use of war imagery
St. Paul saw himself at war
And fellow Christians as well

"Anxiety"
Philippians 2:26-28

Oh, the magnitude of concern
How amazing!
A person's illness raises such a concern
Epaphroditus was the object of much Christian love

Paul was worried
You might even call him
A worry wart
Being anxious to the nth degree

St. Paul was worried about Epaphroditus
He was worried about the Christians in Philippi
He was worried that they were concerned about Epaphroditus
Is there no end to the anxiety?

The apostle's anxiety was borne out of his love
Christian love for fellow Christians
A model of the kind of love that can exist among Christians
Across the racial and ethnic divide

The respected leader
Was concerned that his sheep be comforted
That every caution be taken to allay their fears
Epaphroditus shared in the concern of St. Paul

What does this teach about Christian leadership?
A good Christian leader worries
He worries about his sheep like it is his business
Like there is no tomorrow

A Christian leader obsesses about his flock
Their well-being
This concern occupies a central place in this thought
His whole life

The bond between Christians
Certainly greater than the bond among natural family members
For this bond is forever
We will spend eternity with fellow Christians

So, Christian leaders
Worry about your flock as St. Paul did
Pray for them
Be concerned for their weal

H.C. Kim

"Honor Men Like Him"
Philippians 2:29-30

What kind of people should Christians honor?
People who risk their lives for Gospel work
This is a dictate of St. Paul
It certainly is a value in Christianity to risk one's life for Christ

Deny yourself
Take up your cross
And follow me
Words of Jesus Christ ring forth

It is a call to self-sacrifice
It is a call to be willing to die for Christ
It is a call to discipleship
Of revolutionary proportions

Only natural it is
For Christians to want to give up their lives for Christ
For Christ gave up His all
To die for us

But the flesh is weak
Unfortunately, not all Christians are so bold for the Lord
So stand out the few who willingly risk their lives for Christ
They are examples for all Christians to follow

It is important to encourage Christians to honor
Those who risk their lives for Christ
The saints who have been martyred for their Christian faith
Those who serve the Lord full-time, having given up worldly comforts

St. Paul's words
Honor men like him
Ring forth
All through Christendom

Just like on Memorial Day
We remember the soldiers who fell in battle
Just like we honor soldiers on Veterans' Day
We must make an effort to remember the soldiers of Christ

"Value In Repetition"
Philippians 3:1

A laconic person
Perhaps he was
St. Paul
That is

But he certainly
Repeated
The message
Over and over again

Why?
One may ask
What's the purpose?
It is possible to inquire

For
The Apostle
Reveled in
The Gospel

It was
Joyful
For St. Paul
To repeat

Gospel is
Good News
Truth from the
Source of Truth

Not only that
There was another reason
Purpose dear to Paul
A goal of spiritual dimensions

The repetition was
Strategic
Like a good commander in battle
Paul wanted the soldiers of Christ to win

The good Apostle notes
It is a safeguard for you!
St. Paul wanted to protect his
Flock

Does the Saint
Reveal his educational objective?
Pedagogical philosophy?
His earnest desire for the Kingdom of Christ?

"Watch Out For Those Dogs!"
Philippians 3:2-3

Here he goes again!
St. Paul is warning about the Jews
Who boast about circumcision
And about being the people of God

No equivocal language
Does the Apostle use
In his disdain of them
Those Dogs!

Flat out
The Christian leader defies
The Jewish claim
He drives a spear through the Jewish pride

We are the circumcision
St. Paul argues
We Christians
That is

Christians are the
True circumcision
Followers of Christ are the
True people of God

St. Paul does not want
Confusion
He tries to dispel the notion
That Jews might earn salvation through their tradition

True circumcision
Is not taking off of the foreskin
From the body
Corruptible

The true people of God
Worship by the Spirit of God
Glory in Christ Jesus
Put no confidence in the flesh

St. Paul calls
The Jews emphasizing circumcision
As mutilators of the flesh
As if they were some criminals

Watch out for them!
The Apostle warns
As if they were like lions
Looking for someone to devour

They are
Doers of evil!
St. Paul paints a nasty picture
Of those Jews who value circumcision

"Legalistic Righteousness"
Philippians 3:4-6

How Martin Luther must have
Reveled
In St. Paul's
Attack
Of legalistic righteousness!

There seems to be
Nothing
That offends the Apostle more
Than legalistic righteousness
False claim to salvation

St. Paul gives his personal testimony
His claim to Jewishness
He was circumcised on the eighth day
He belonged to the tribe of Benjamin
Hebrew of Hebrews

Furthermore
Before conversion to Christianity
Paul kept the law like a good Pharisee
Persecuted Christians with zeal
These were signs of Jewishness for St. Paul

All this legal righteousness
St. Paul sees as a source of shame
The life of the past
That was opposed to the new life
In Christ Jesus

His Jewishness
Was a part of life according to the flesh
Legalistic observance
That opposed the True Spirit of the Living God
The Holy Trinity

No
No longer
Did St. Paul
Feel pride in all those things
As before becoming Christian

"Past Profit Is Current Loss"
Philippians 3:7-8

Who says that persecuting Christians
Isn't a profitable enterprise?

For St. Paul before conversion to Christianity
He benefited from harassing Christians

There was a price on the heads of Christians
They probably considered it fun to persecute them

The Jews were zealous in persecuting Christians
St. Paul before conversion was, too

This and all other benefits which St. Paul experienced
Before coming to the saving knowledge in Christ Jesus

The Apostle now considered them as loss
"Past profit is current loss"

Why?
For the sake of Christ

Knowing Jesus Christ personally is that great
That all other things pale in comparison

Nothing in this world
Honor, wealth, titles, possessions matter

When compared with the salvation in Christ we have
The eternal life that Christ paid for with His blood

St. Paul considers all as
Rubbish

Like trash
Are the valuable things of this world

Personally meaningless
Are those which held so much import in the past

Effectively unattached
Did St. Paul feel towards that which pulled him before

The Apostle was liberated
He tasted the freedom in Christ

"Righteousness By Faith"
Philippians 3:9

The just shall live by faith
So the hail of the Reformation
We are not made righteous in God's eyes
By what we do
But by faith which is the gift of God

The righteousness that comes from God
Is by faith in Christ Jesus
Who died on the cross
An atoning death
In substitution for all who would believe in Him

There is no justification
In the law
Observing the law
Will not buy your salvation
Only Christ's blood redeems

To be found in Christ
Is only possible through faith
Faith is unseen
It is an implicit trust in
Christ's redeeming work on the Cross

To be a member of the people of God
One must believe that Christ is God
This faith comes through the
Irresistible Grace
Of the Lord Jesus Christ

When a person is
Effectively Called
She will be joyful
In accepting the gift of God
Faith in Jesus Christ

Righteousness comes by faith
In Jesus Christ
For Christ has paid it all
And all to Him belong
Those who believe that He is God

H.C. Kim

"I Want To Know Christ"
Philippians 3:10-11

Intimate relationship
Longed for thoroughly
Wanting to imitate
Christ the personal Savior
That's what St. Paul wanted

To know Christ
What does it all mean?
For St. Paul
The answer is all in the
Person and life of Jesus Christ

The power of His resurrection
Victory over sin and death
The triumphant hour
When the atoning sacrifice was completed
He has crushed the Serpent's head!

St. Paul wanted to taste
For sure, in perpetuity
The power of Christ's resurrection
That completed the propitiatory work on the cross
And what success it was!

Christ's resurrection was foretold
In the Old Testament and the New
It's completion was the fulfillment
Of the promise of God
God is love!

But
Oh, how He suffered
Tortured and battered
Dragged to the cross
With thorns for a crown

Even the sufferings of Christ
St. Paul wanted to know
He wanted to deny himself
Take up his cross and follow Him
As commanded by the Savior

115

Christ's suffering
One of rejection
Humiliation
Filled with sorrow
Pain

The Apostle knew
It was all for him
That Christ suffered
And died
He was grateful

The leader of the Christian church
Wanted to follow in the footsteps of Christ
Even to the point of death
St. Paul testifies
He wants to become like Christ in His death

Oh, to long for death
To die like Jesus did
To the glory of the Triune God
What lofty goal
Of the Christian missionary

There is life after death
Eternal life for those
Justified in the blood of the Cross
St. Paul had confidence
In his faith in the Lord Jesus

The Apostle knew
That resurrection awaited him
Were he to give up his life for Christ
There was eternal life waiting for him
Along with the crown of righteousness

To know Christ
What a desire
Bubbling inside of the missionary
Who has given his all
To be in Christ's all

"Looking Forward To Glorification"
Philippians 3:12

Glorification
The final step in the process of salvation
Started with predestination
Effectual calling
Justification
And sanctification

That is the goal toward which
St. Paul is running
The Apostle knows
Christ has procured the prize
Already for him on the cross
But in obedience he runs

The Christian presses on
Whatever the environment
Despite the hardship
However he feels
In weakness and in strength
The final destination looms large in her eyes

Press on, brother!
Press on, sister!
For the final glorification awaits
Oh, how wonderful that day will be!
We will be joined together with Christ
And we will reign forever with Him

"To Win The Prize"
Philippians 3:13-14

I press on towards the goal
To obtain the prize
Heavenward
I go
Testifies St. Paul

I forget what is behind
It was a past filled with
Persecution of Christians
Observance of the Law
No longer I desire that

Only forward
Toward eternal life
Glorification
That the Lord Jesus has prepared
I step to the beat of His drums

Press on!
One could almost hear
The cry of St. Paul
Sincere earnestness
In his voice

The Apostle
Saw himself
As one of the believers
Followers of Christ
Who needed to press on towards the goal

Oh
Wonderful day it certainly will be!
Marvelous is
That day
When we reach our glorification

Completion of a long journey
Race that was fraught with difficulties
Tribulations overcome
The good fight
Won

H.C. Kim

To win the prize
That the Triune God
Has prepared for his believers
The Christians
I strain towards the goal

"Mature Christians Should Think Like Me"
Philippians 3:15

What is St. Paul saying here?
He is propounding the mature view
All who do not agree are
Immature Christians
And they should change their views

The Apostle is not accommodating
Different views that other believers held
St. Paul simply argues
That those who think differently
Are mistaken and they should correct themselves

The leader of the Christian church
Had authority from the Lord Jesus Christ
He was eager to guard the Gospel Truth
To defend the Church of Jesus Christ
To fight the good fight against the enemies of Christ

St. Paul ruthlessly attacked Judaism
The greatest threat to Christianity
Which could subvert from within
He did not show mercy in his attack
The Apostle shamed converts from Judaism who tried to change
    the Gospel

St. Paul spoke with authority
For he knew his teaching was grounded in the Gospel
Jesus had attacked Judaism
Emphasized salvation only through belief in Him
The Apostle was merely following his LORD

Mature Christians should think like me!
That's what St. Paul is saying here
In effect
Those who do not
Have long way to go

Who knows the reason why some are kept from maturity?
Sin has corrupted one's logic
It is not in accord with God's view
As expounded in the Bible
Oh, the damage that the Fall has wrought!

Believers are called
Yes they are heralded
To transform their mind
Conform their views
To the Word of God

"Enemies Of The Cross"
Philippians 3:16-18

Many there are
Who live as
Enemies of the
Cross of Jesus Christ
St. Paul warns

Who are these people?
Those who belittle the redemptive work
Those who do not emphasize that
Jesus is the only way to salvation
Jews who say Christ is unnecessary for salvation

St. Paul constantly attacks the
Enemies of Christ
How many times does he attack
Judaism?
Constantly

St. Paul is concerned with
Protecting the Church of Christ
To fight against those who try to destroy it
From within
And from without

St. Paul wants believers to
Follow his example
And those like him
Stephen who was killed by Jews
Also attacked Judaism

Judaism is false religion
Jewish leaders rejected the
True Messiah
Jesus Christ
For this they are condemned

Not being ruthless in attack of the
Enemies of Christ
Is disobeying the Word of God
The commandment of the Holy One
To His saints

Being holy
In Christianity
Necessarily requires
Attacking the enemies of Christ
For instance, Judaism

Anything
That tries to subvert
Christianity
And the message of the Cross
Must be attacked

St. Paul
Does not cease
From this important
Christian work
He calls Christians to follow in his steps

"The Destiny Of The Enemies Of The Cross"
Philippians 3:19

Enemies of the Cross
Will be
Destroyed
That is their destiny
St. Paul prophesies

For the enemies of the
Cross of Jesus Christ
Do not care about the Gospel Truth
They care about the world
And what it could provide

Was not St. Paul one of them before?
He before conversion to Christianity
Went around persecuting Christians
It gave him prestige in the Jewish community
It brought him honor and even profit

How many are there, today
Who are willing to let
Christians be attacked
Because they want to protect their possessions
And their well-being?

Has it become profitable
To stand against
The teachings of Christ
That the only way to salvation
Is through belief in Jesus Christ as God?

Does holding the Gospel Truth position
That all other religions are false
Bring disadvantage for the true Christian
Who does not want to compromise
The Word of God?

Are there laws being passed
Which try to ensure
That Christians will not be able to say
That other religions are false
And that Christianity is the only true religion?

Who are the enemies of the Cross
Who advance the anti-Christian message?
Who has bowed down to Satan
Who promises riches?
Who stands against the Gospel Truth?

These enemies of Christ
Want to stroke the egos of those
Who hate Christ
Who hold wealth
And power

Enemies of Christ
Will come to
Destruction
That is the promise of God
That St. Paul proclaims

"Our Citizenship Is In Heaven"
Philippians 3:20-21

Everyone you know probably holds a citizenship
Some country on this earth which claims her allegiance
The benefit of belonging to that country is hers
Probably the ills as well

Where is your citizenship?
Let's rephrase that
Where is your primary citizenship?
Primary allegiance?

For St. Paul
The citizenship of the Christian
Is in Heaven
In the Kingdom of Christ

The benefit of belonging to
Christ's realm
Is obvious
Eternal life is waiting

However
There are
"Disadvantages"
As well

A Christian
Will necessarily suffer
Persecution
For the Truth

A follower of Christ
Is called to deny oneself
Take up her cross
And follow Jesus Christ

One redeemed in Christ
Is called to preach the Gospel
In season
And out of season

The heavy responsibility of
Standing up for the Truth
And defending it is
On her shoulders

It is all worth it
For Christ has bought
Our salvation
With His blood shed on the cross

We cry out Abba Father
We have reconciliation with the
Triune God
On account of Christ's propitiatory sacrifice

How seriously
Do Christians of today
View their citizenship in
Heaven?

Is it more important than
Holding a USA passport?
Claiming oneself to be a citizen of Canada?
Your beloved X country?

Do we fulfill our obligations
As Christians
Citizens of the Almighty
Living God?

Are we even
Aware
Of our allegiance
To Christ?

"My Joy And Crown"
Philippians 4:1

Oh what flattery!
You may say cynically
St. Paul lays on the sauce!
But he was being sincere
My friend
In his affection for the Christian believers

For the Apostle
The Christians in Philippi
Were a source of joy
He expressed honestly how he felt
In encouragement
As a testimony

Christian leaders would do well
To learn from this style
Praising Christians
For qualities that are true
Is not vain vagary
It is an effective way to spur someone towards good

St. Paul
As it is clear
Was never holding back punches
In attacking the enemies of Christ
But he also never hesitated
To offer praise

The Apostle
Encouraged
Spured the believers of Christ
On
Towards
Greater loyalty to the Lord Jesus

As much as
He attacked
With ferociousness
Those who sought
To water down the Gospel
Or destroy it

"Agree With Each Other In The Lord"
Philippians 4:2-3

Christian harmony
A perennial concern of St. Paul
For it aids in the spreading of the Gospel
A kingdom divided cannot stand
Rings true the Word of Jesus of Nazareth

How wonderful it is
When Christians live in harmony
Harmony with non-Christians is
Impossible
Because they oppose Jesus our Lord

Non-Christians are going to Hell
Jews
Hindus
Buddhists
Muslims

True harmony is only possible
Between Christians
And how important it is!
St. Paul works to create unity
Among Christian believers

The Apostle pleads with
Euodia
And Syntyche
To agree with each other in the Lord
Jesus Christ the Savior God

And how St. Paul
Exhorts
Encourages
Saints in Philippi
To encourage them in the same way

One in Christ
For those who accept Jesus
As Lord and Savior
Christ has paid it all
With his precious blood

The Christian Spirit

Although we should discourage
Unity with non-Christians
That compromises the Gospel Truth
We must encourage
Harmony among Christian believers

H.C. Kim

"The Transcendent Peace Of God"
Philippians 4:4-7

Joy
Prayer
Gentleness
Thanksgiving
How precious they are!

With faith in Christ
The transcendent peace of God is yours
It surpasses all understanding
Because it is spiritual peace
That the world does not understand

How important it is to rejoice
Rejoice in the Lord always!
For again I say rejoice!
For Christ has redeemed me
From the eternal holocaust in Hell

Joy exuberant
Thinking about the eternity
We will spend in Heaven
With our Lord and Savior
Jesus Christ

We could be gentle
In the Spirit of God
Reveling in the harmony
Created between us and God the Father
Through the mediating work of the Cross

Anxious?
No room for that
Because we have God on our side
All we need to do is trust in Him
In prayer and supplication

Yes, the transcendent peace of God
Is given as a gift
To the Christian believer
Sure, we do not deserve it
But God is gracious

"God Of Spiritual Peace Be With You"
Philippians 4:8-9

Thoughts flowing like a stream
How crowded our minds are
With observations all around us
Things we see and hear
Confusion often rises

In a world
Filled with impurities
Imperfections
Faults
Wrongs

Thoughts
That can't be described as
Noble
Can enter
And do

Oh,
What a struggle it is for
A Christian
To purify one's mind
And heart

Precisely
Isn't that the encouragement of St. Paul?
To think on
Pure things
Noble things

An active process
It certainly is
To seek good things
Those that are pleasing to God
How could we pursue them?

Like torrents
In a fierce storm
The currents go the other way
The world embraces
Not that what God wants

Like salmon
Swimming against the stream
Uphill
With its last ounce of strength
Holding on to its resolution

We Christians are exhorted
To hold onto
All that is lovely
True
Admirable

In our thoughts
Make deposits
Of sparkling
Values
Christian

Meditating on the
Teaching of the Apostle
What we have received
In the Word of God
For the Truth shall set you free
\

Put it into practice!
Both an admonition
And encouragement
A duty
A calling

I think, therefore I am
Goes a famous saying
Striving to think about Christian things
Perhaps, this is a sign of being a true Christian?
And also to do that which we have learned

The promise
God of peace will be with you
Spiritual peace will be yours
God's comforting hand will be upon you
Grace be with you

"Expression"
Philippians 4:10

What good is it?
You may ask
What good is it
If you are concerned
But do not show it?

Sure
There is value in it
It is a good thing to be concerned
Even if
One does not show it

Particularly if
One prays for the other
And the concerns which he may
Have
Real good can come about through prayer

But how much better it is!
When the concern is expressed
Words of comfort
Like sweet honey
Delivered as if as a gift

St. Paul
Reflects on his experience
The encouragement he felt
In hearing the concern of
The Christians in Philippi

I rejoice greatly in the Lord Jesus
Because you have renewed
Your concern for me
I am sure you were concerned for me before
But you probably did not have the chance to show it

The Apostle was a
Human being
Who needed encouragement
The followers of Christ in Philippi
Provided the needed joy

H.C. Kim

What a blessing it is!
When we have believers so concerned
Itinerant missionaries
Working together with Christian communities
To spread the Gospel of Jesus Christ

"Contentment In Need"
Philippians 4:11-12

Satisfaction
Always a property of the blessed
Being able to find
Contentment
Even in need
Oh, how precious it is!

St. Paul was one of the fortunate ones
Who found contentment in need
He knew what is was to lack
As well as what it was to
Have

Being joyful when you have
Could be much easier
Than finding peace
When you do not
Have

Even though
To have does not necessarily
Bring happiness
Some wealthy people commit suicide
Oh, how sad it is!

To be happy when you lack nothing
Could be difficult as well
For with possessions come worries
Some even say those who lack
Could even be truly happy

To be content in both cases
When one has and one has not
That is a blessing to be enjoyed by few
St. Paul was one of them
He could truly be happy

Hungry
Lacking food
Not having money for sustenance
Poor
It could be agitating

H.C. Kim

The Apostle experienced it
He knew what it was all about
But even then
He was content
Because he found joy in Christ

Well fed
Abundance of food
Tasty delights
Sumptuous to the eyes
St. Paul experienced that too

The Apostle experienced it
He knew what it was all about
But even then
He was content
Because he found joy in Christ

"Through Him Who Gives Me Strength"
Philippians 4:13

Through Him
All things are possible
Jesus Christ
Who is the Creator of the world
God the Son

I can do anything
Through Him
The Creator God
Who gives me
Strength

How wonderful it is to put faith in Him!
The Lord Jesus Christ
Not only did He save me from my sins
Gave me eternal life in
Heaven

Christ Jesus makes possible
Even those things
That seem
Impossible
For human beings

All things are possible with God
Have faith
My friend
Trust in the Lord
As St. Paul did

The Triune God will open the way
For He is the Creator
Sustainer
Preserver
Of all things

Our Lord is good
And His love endures
Forever
Trust in Him
My friend

"Financial Support"
Philippians 4:14-17

Saints in Philippi
Will be
Remembered
Forever
For being St. Paul's financial supporters

A dollar goes only so far
So one says
But in the case of St. Paul
Every cent went to
Gospel work

The Apostle was grateful for the support
He mentions with thanksgiving
And it was encapsulated in the Bible
For generations to see
The Word of God

Yes
The Christian Church
Needs great ministers of the Gospel
For the Word of God must be proclaimed
By effective vessels

But
There needs to be
Supporters of Christian work
Those who are willing to toil and earn
And contribute to the cause

It is when there is harmony
A wonderful combination of
Preacher
And financial supporters
That the Gospel work can go forth effectively

Will you be that supporter?
Whose financial help
Supports Christian ministry
So that people can come to know
Jesus Christ as their personal Lord and Savior

"Fragrant Offering"
Philippians 4:18

Financial contribution to St. Paul's ministry
Described as a fragrant offering
Acceptable sacrifice
Some Christians would object to it
Don't you think?

How dare St. Paul
Equate donation to
His ministry with
Sacrifice to God
The Lord Jesus Christ?

But the Apostle did
Setting a precedent
For other Christian ministers
To equate donation
With Christian offering

Yes, indeed
Financial contribution
To Gospel work
Is like offering up a sacrifice
To the Triune God

It is an important part of Christian work
It is needed to spread the Gospel
We must follow St. Paul's example
In the way we perceive donation to
Christian missions work

"Glorious Riches In Christ"
Philippians 4:19

Who says that the Lord does not bless materially?
To those who contribute financially to
Christ's work
Spreading of the Word of Christ
The Lord will bless even financially

Storing up treasures in Heaven
One could even be blessed here on earth
The Lord owns this world
He can give whatever He wants
To whomever He wants

The treasure stores of Heaven
Gates could be opened
So that the wealth could come pouring in
To those who have made a Heaven investment
By supporting Christian ministry

So, don't be afraid
To pray to the living God in Heaven
To make you a millionaire
In order that you might support a Christian work
Financially and effectively

We need rich Christians
To help with the financial aspects of
Christian work
So go on pray
The Lord will answer

But always have the attitude
Even when I am not wealthy
I will give for the work of the Lord
I will tithe my earning
And give fragrant sacrifice to the Lord Jesus

"Glory Forever And Ever"
Philippians 4:20

Why do I love God?
Because He has redeemed me from my sin

Why do I glorify God?
Because He is God and is owed glory

Why do I worship God?
Because He demands worship

Why do I preach about God?
Because of the salvation that I have in Christ

Why do I pray?
Because it is a joy to talk with God the Father

Why do I read the Bible?
Because it is the Word of God and a gift of God

Why do I share the love of Christ?
Because Christ commands it

Why do I take up my cross?
Because Christ took up the cross that saved me from Hell

Why do I do what I do?
Because I have been bought at the price of Jesus' blood

To the Triune God
Be the Glory forever and ever

"Caesar's Household"
Philippians 4:21-23

Ho!
There were believers in Christ
Among those who belonged to
Caesar's household!
Christianity is growing!

It is a picture of how effective
The Gospel missions work was
It had infiltrated the leadership
The Ruler's household
Pagan ruler's household

It is like a member of the
Fundamentalist Hindu government
Believing in Jesus Christ as Lord and Savior
The Prime Minister of the BJP Party in India
Having a family member being born again in Jesus

How wonderful that would be
I bet India's Christians would rejoice
And celebrate the goodness of the Lord Jesus
Perhaps some are preaching the Gospel to them even now
Or strategizing to

Power of Christian missions
Converted the Roman Emperor
And the Roman Empire
To Christianity
Such is the power of the one true living God

This can happen in India
Or any other country in the world
With dedicated Christians
Who love the Lord
And are fearless in their Christian witness

Glory only to God in the Highest
Jesus Christ is the one true living God
God the Son is in eternal fellowship with
God the Father and God the Spirit
All honor be to the Trinity

www.ingramcontent.com/pod-product-compliance
Lightning Source LLC
Chambersburg PA
CBHW051831040426
42447CB00006B/482